BARMOUTH TO PWLLHELI

Vic Mitchell and Keith Smith

MP Middleton Press

Front cover: A train for Pwllheli is on the left on 26th May 1958, as 2-6-2Ts nos 4599 and 4560 wait to depart from Portmadoc. The smaller signal was for Beddgelert Siding. (G.Adams/ M.J.Stretton coll.)

Back cover: Nos 37427 and 37428 run round the empty stock of the 07.30 from Euston at Pwllheli on 19th July 1986, the last year of trains from London. (B.Robbins)

Pwllheli's first station. (A.Rhodes coll.)

Published June 2009

ISBN 978 1 906008 53 6

© *Middleton Press, 2009*

Design Deborah Esher
Typesetting Barbara Mitchell

Published by
        Middleton Press
        Easebourne Lane
        Midhurst
        West Sussex
        GU29 9AZ
Tel: 01730 813169
Fax: 01730 812601
Email: info@middletonpress.co.uk
www.middletonpress.co.uk

Printed in the United Kingdom by Henry Ling Limited, at the Dorset Press, Dorchester, DT1 1HD

INDEX

ACKNOWLEDGEMENTS

We are very grateful for the assistance received from many of those mentioned in the credits also to D.Allan, A.R.Carder, L.Crosier, G.Croughton, F.Hornby, S.C.Jenkins, J.Keylock, N.Langridge, B.Lewis, D.T.Rowe, Mr D. and Dr S.Salter, T.Walsh, G.Williams and in particular, our always supportive wives, Barbara Mitchell and Janet Smith.

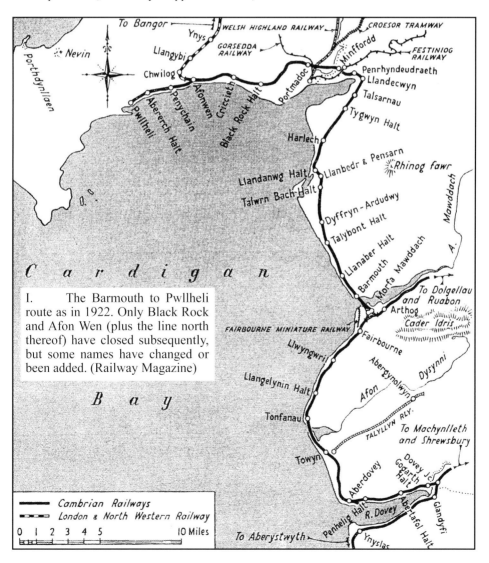

I.   The Barmouth to Pwllheli route as in 1922. Only Black Rock and Afon Wen (plus the line north thereof) have closed subsequently, but some names have changed or been added. (Railway Magazine)

GEOGRAPHICAL SETTING

Most of the route is on the coastal plain, which overlies the very old sedimentary rocks described as Cambrian. North of Minffordd is a notable extrusion of once soft hot rock, but only half of the hill remains now, owing to quarrying activity. Used for road surfacing, the igneous rock is known as syenite.

Two important rivers are crossed. The first is the Dwyryd, south of Penrhyndeudraeth and the other follows in about two miles. This is the Glaslyn and its estuary was reclaimed from the sea in the early 19th century. The dam is known as The Cob and it carries the A497 and the 1836 Festiniog Railway. This and other narrow gauge lines provided our route with much mineral traffic until World War II, mainly slate.

Welsh spelling and hyphenation has varied over the years and so we have generally used the most recent form as have the railways.

The maps are to the scale of 25ins to 1 mile, with north at the top, unless otherwise indicated.

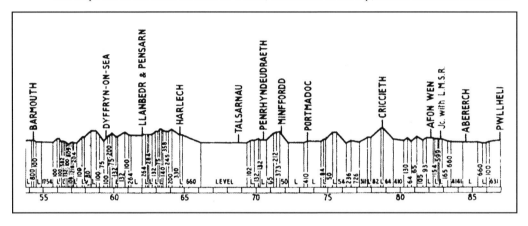

HISTORICAL BACKGROUND

The Newtown & Machynlleth Railway was authorised in 1857 and opened west to Borth on 1st July 1863. Completion to Aberystwyth was undertaken by the Aberystwyth & Welsh Coast Railway on 23rd June 1864 and all these lines became part of the new Cambrian Railways in 1864-65.

The A&WCR extended northwards by opening the Aberdovey to Llyngwril section on 24th October 1863. The CR finished the route in stages. Llyngwril north to Penmaenpool (two miles west of Dolgelley) followed on 3rd July 1865 and it was extended to that town in 1868, where it made a connection with the new Bala & Dolgelley Railway.

Barmouth Junction (Morfa Mawddach from 1960) to Pwllheli opened on 3rd June 1867 and Dovey Junction (Glandovey Junction until 1904) to Aberdovey followed on 14th August of that year. The line south from Carnarvon (as it then was) to Afon Wen also opened in 1867, this being operated by the London & North Western Railway from 1870. The Cambrian Railways became part of the Great Western Railway in 1922.

With the advent of nationalisation, all lines in the area became part of the Western Region of British Railways on 1st January 1948. The route was transferred to the London Midland Region on 17th June 1963.

Closure of the route was threatened and the Cambrian Coast Line Action Group was formed in 1971. It was extremely active and victory was achieved in July 1974. However, in April 1980 Barmouth Bridge was declared unsafe, but further campaigning resulted in repairs during a brief closure period and its reopening in May 1981. The group organised Sunday trains that Summer. Subsequently most level crossings were automated as an economy measure.

An important event in the history of the line took place in October 1988, when a Radio Electronic Token Block system was introduced, the control being at Machynlleth.

Privatisation resulted in Central Trains operating services from 2nd March 1997. However, after reorganisation in October 2001, Wales & Borders became the franchisee. Arriva Trains Wales took over in December 2003.

The European Rail Traffic Management System was introduced in experimental form in 2008, prior to its use on the Thameslink route in Central London.

PASSENGER SERVICES

The table shows the number of down trains, but excludes those running on limited weekdays only. There were one or two others between Afon Wen and Pwllheli, which originated at Bangor or Euston.

Through trains (or coaches) from London via Barmouth were known as the "Cambrian Coast Express" from 1927 and ran from Paddington until 1967, war years excepted. The London terminus then became Euston, although the train name was not used again until 1986. The service was Summer only and later restricted to Saturdays only and the name was changed to the "Snowdonian".

	Barmouth to Pwllheli		Portmadoc to Pwllheli Extras on
	Weekdays	Sundays	Weekdays
1869	3	1	2
1885	5	1	6
1895	3	1	5
1904	8	1	3
1925	4	0	4
1940	5	1	0
1955	8	0	2
1971	6	0	0
1985	7	0	0
2009	8	1	0

August 1940

Railway timetable: MACHYNLLETH, BARMOUTH, and PWLLHELI.

MACHYNLLETH, TOWYN, BARMOUTH, and PWLLHELI

Miles		Week Days																												Sundays		
		a.m	a.m		a.m	a.m	a.m	a.m	a.m	a.m		p.m		a.m		p.m	p.m	p.m	p.m	p.m	p.m	p.m	p.m	p.m	p.m	p.m	p.m	p.m	p.m	a.m		
—	**Machynlleth** .... dep	..	..	..	..	6 50	..	8 5	..	..	..	..	..	1045	..	..	..	1 18	..	..	..	3 30	..	..	..	5 30	..	6 55	..	9 0	..	..
3¾	Dovey Junction ..... arr	..	..	..	..	..	..	8 12	..	..	..	..	..	1052	..	..	..	1 25	..	..	..	3 37	..	..	..	5 37	..	7 2	..	..	..	..
—	184 ABERYSTWYTH .... dep	..	..	..	..	..	..	7 30	..	..	..	..	..	9 55	..	..	..	1250	..	..	..	2 30	..	..	..	4 40	..	6 0	..	..	..	..
—	Dovey Junction .... dep	..	..	..	..	..	..	8 15	..	..	..	..	..	11 5	..	..	..	1 35	..	..	..	3 38	..	..	..	5 40	..	7 5	..	..	..	..
5½	Gogarth Halt	..	..	..	..	..	..	8 19	..	..	..	..	..	11 9	..	..	..	1 39	..	..	..	Uu	..	..	..	..	..	7 11	..	..	..	..
7	Abertafol Halt	..	..	..	..	..	..	8 25	..	..	..	..	..	1115	..	..	..	1 45	..	..	..	3 47	..	..	..	5 48	..	Uu	..	..	..	..
9	Penhelig Halt	..	..	..	..	7 11	..	8 30	..	..	..	..	..	1120	..	..	..	1 50	..	..	..	3 52	..	..	..	5 54	..	7 19	..	9 19	..	..
9¾	**Aberdovey**	..	..	..	..	7 15	..	8 33	..	..	..	..	..	1124	..	..	..	1 53	..	..	..	3 56	..	..	..	5 58	..	7 24	..	9 23	..	..
13½	Towyn	..	..	..	..	7 27	..	8 47	..	..	..	..	..	1136	..	..	..	2 0	..	..	..	4 6	..	..	..	6 9	..	7 32	..	9 31	..	..
15¾	Tonfanau	..	..	..	..	7 33	..	8 54	..	..	..	..	..	1143	..	..	..	2 6	..	..	..	4 11	..	..	..	6 14	..	7 38	..	9 36	..	..
18	Llangelynin Halt	..	..	..	..	..	..	8 58	..	..	..	..	..	1148	..	..	..	2 10	..	..	..	4Ƶ15	..	..	..	6 18	..	7 43	..	..	..	..
20	Llwyngwril	..	..	..	..	7 41	..	9 3	..	..	..	..	..	1155	..	..	..	2 18		..	..	4 19	..	..	..	6 22	..	7 49	..	9 44	..	..
22¾	Fairbourne	..	..	..	..	7 48	..	9 10	..	..	..	TC from Liverpool (L. St.) dep. 7E50, 7§42 a.m. From Bangor dep. 11 30 a.m., page 517	..	12 3	..	..	..	2 26		..	..	4 26	..	..	..	6 30	..	7 57	..	9 52	..	..
23¾	Barmouth Junction. arr	..	..	..	..	7 51	..	9 13	..	..	..		..	12 6	..	..	..	2 29		..	..	4 30	..	..	..	6 32	..	8 0	..	9 55	..	..
33	187 Dolgelley .... arr	..	..	..	..	..	(3)	9Ħ46	..	..	..		..	1 36	..	..	(3)	3 2	Except Saturdays and School Holidays	..	..	6Y12	..	..	..	7 41	(3)	9§38	..	..	..	..
	dep	..	..	..	..	..	8 30	..	9 30	1138	..		..	..	..	..	1 45	..		..	..	..	4 2	4 58	..	4 58	6 18	..	8 55	..	..	..
—	Barmouth Junction. dep	..	..	..	..	7 52	8 52	9 14	10 0	12 3	..		..	12 9	..	..	2 7	2 30		..	..	4 31	4 25	5 20	..	6 33	6 40	8 2	9 18	9 56	..	..
25½	**Barmouth** ...... arr	..	..	..	..	7 57	8 57	9 19	10 5	12 8	..		..	1214	..	..	2 12	2 36		..	..	4 36	4 30	5 25	..	6 38	6 45	8 7	9 23	10 1	..	..
	dep	..	..	..	..	8 10	..	9 25	..	..	..		..	..	..	1220	..	2 40		..	3 50	..	4 44	5 30	..	6 50	—	8 12	..	..	..	..
27	Llanaber Halt	..	..	..	..	..	..	9 28	..	..	..		..	..	..	1227	..	..		..	3 54	..	4 48	..	..	6 54	..	8 16	..	..	..	..
29¼	Talybont Halt	..	..	..	..	..	..	9 32	..	..	..		..	..	..	1232	..	..		..	3 58	..	4 52	..	..	6 58	..	8 21	..	..	..	..
30¼	Dyffryn-Ardudwy	..	..	..	..	8 18	..	9 35	..	..	..		..	..	..	1236	..	2 50		..	4 2	..	4 55	5 39	..	7 2	..	8 29	..	..	..	..
32¾	Talwrn Bach Halt	..	..	..	..	8 23	..	9 40	..	..	..		..	..	..	1241	..	..		..	4 7	..	4 59	..	..	7 7	..	8 34	..	..	..	..
33½	Llanbedr and Pensarn	..	..	..	..	8 30	..	9 43	..	..	..		..	..	..	1243	..	2 57		..	4 11	..	5 3	5 44	From Bangor dep. 5 39 p.m., page 517	7 10	..	8 37	..	..	..	..
34	Llandanwg Halt	..	From Bangor dep. 5 30 a.m., page 517	..	..	8 32	..	9 47	..	..	..		..	..	..	1247	..	..		From Bangor dep. 2 52 p.m., page 517	4 13	..	5 7	..		..	..	8 39	..	..	..	..
36	**Harlech**	..		..	..	8 41	..	9 52	..	..	..		..	..	..	1254	..	3 5			4 19	..	5 13	5 51		7 18	..	8 46	..	..	..	..
38½	Tygwyn Halt	..		..	..	8 46	..	9 56	..	..	..		..	..	..	1259	..	..			4 23	..	5 17	..		7 22	..	8 51	..	..	..	..
39¼	Talsarnau	..		..	..	8 49	..	9 59	..	..	..		..	..	..	1 2	..	3 11			4 26	..	5 20	..		7 25	..	8 54	..	..	..	..
40¼	Llandecwyn Halt	..		..	..	8 54	..	10 3	..	..	..		..	..	..	1 5	..	..			4 30	..	5 25	..		..	..	8 58	..	..	..	..
41½	Penrhyndeudraeth	..		..	..	9 0	..	10 6	..	..	..		..	..	..	1 8	..	3 16	..		4 40	..	5 28	6 5		7 31	..	9 2	..	..	..	..
42½	Minffordd	..		..	..	9 4	..	1010	..	..	..		..	..	..	1 12	..	3 20	..		4 46	..	5 32	Zz		7 35	..	9 6	..	..	..	..
44¾	**Portmadoc** ..... arr	..		..	..	9 8	..	1014	..	..	..		..	..	..	1 16	..	3 25	(3)		4 50	..	5 36	6 14		7 40	..	9 11	..	..	..	..
	dep	6 0		..	7 40	9 10	..	1017	..	..	..		..	..	..	1 20	..	3 27	4 5		4 52	..	5 38	6 15		8 15	..	9 14	..	..	..	..
48½	Black Rock Halt	..		..	..	..	..	Nn	..	..	..		..	..	..	Nn	..	..	..		..	..	..	..		..	..	..	..	..	..	..
49¾	Criccieth	6 12		..	7 51	9 19	..	1030	..	..	..		..	..	..	1 32	..	3 36	4 13		5 1	..	5 45	6 24		8 24	..	9 22	..	..	..	..
53	Afon Wen ..... arr	6 18		..	7 57	9 25	..	1036	..	..	..		..	..	..	1 38	..	3 42	..		5 6	..	5 51	6 30		8 30	..	9 28	..	..	..	..
	dep	6 23	7 9	..	8 2	9 28	..	1040	..	..	..	1255	..	..	..	1 49	..	3 46	..	4 18	5 8	..	5 53	6 32	7 0	8 33	..	9 29	..	..	..	..
54½	Penychain **D**	6 26	7 12	..	8 5	9 31	..	1044	..	..	..	1258	..	..	..	1 52	..	3 49	..	4 21	5 11	..	5 56	6 35	7 3	8 36	..	9 32	..	..	..	..
55¾	Abererch	..	7 15	..	8 8	9 34	..	1047	..	..	..	1 1	..	..	..	1 56	..	3 52	..	4 24	5 14	..	5 59	6 38	7 6	8 39	..	..	..	..	..	..
57¾	**Pwllheli** .... arr	6 35	7 21	..	8 14	9 40	..	1053	..	..	..	1 7	..	..	..	2 2	..	4 0	..	4 30	5 20	..	6 5	6 44	7 12	8 45	..	9 40	..	..	..	..

D For Pwllheli Holiday Camp E Except Saturdays Ħ Third class only **Nn** Calls to pick up or set down passengers. Passengers wishing to alight must give notice to the Guard at previous *stopping* station and those desiring to join should give necessary hand signal to the Driver § Saturdays only **TC** Through Carriages **Uu** Calls to set down passengers on notice being given by the passenger to the Guard at Dovey Junc. Y First and Third class except Sats. Third Class only on Sats. Ƶ Except Saturdays and School Holidays **Zz** Calls to set down passengers on notice being given by the passenger to the Guard at Barmouth § Third class only; arr. 10 6 p.m. on Saturdays (3) Third class only

January 1955

May 1984

Miles		BHX					C SX				C SX					C SX		A SO					D		
—	Barmouth ....76 d	....	....	....	....	....	0817	....	1030k	....	1145p	....	1333b	....	....	1521	....	....	....	1805n	....	....	....	....	....
—	Pwllheli ....76 d	..	..	0800n	..	..		..	1015b	..	1215	..	1215b	..	..	1500	..	1500	..	1645n	..	..	..	..	..
—	Harlech ....76 d	....	....	....	....	....	0847	....	1100k	....	1208p	....	1356b	....	....	1549	....		....	1832n	....	....	....	....	....
—	Porthmadog Harbour ....510 d	..	..	0840n	..	..	0950	..	1220b	..	1310	..	1455b	..	..	1635	..	1635c	..	1900n	..	..	..	..	..
—	Minffordd ....510, 76 d	....	....	0849n	....	....	0959	....	1229b	....	1319	....	1504b	....	....	1644	....	1644c	....	1900n	....	....	....	....	....
0	**Blaenau Ffestiniog** ....d	0700	..	0945	..	..	1105	..	1330	..	1450	..	1625	..	..	1748	..	1748	..	2020	..	..	2142	..	..
5	Roman Bridge ....d	0711x	....	0956x	....	....	1116x	....	1341x	....	1501x	....	1636x	....	....	1759x	....	1759x	....	2031x	....	....	2153x	....	....
6½	Dolwyddelan ....d	0715x	..	1000x	..	..	1120x	..	1345x	..	1505x	..	1640x	..	..	1803x	..	1803x	..	2035x	..	..	2157x	..	..
8½	Pont-y-Pant ....d	0719x	....	1004x	....	....	1124x	....	1349x	....	1509x	....	1644x	....	....	1807x	....	1807x	....	2039x	....	....	2201x	....	....
12½	Betws-y-Coed ....d	0728	..	1013	..	..	1133	..	1358	..	1518	..	1653	..	..	1816	..	1816	..	2048	..	..	2210	..	..
16½	Llanrwst ....d	0735	....	1020	....	....	1140	....	1405	....	1525	....	1700	....	....	1825	....	1825	....	2055	....	....	2217	....	....
19½	Dolgarrog ....d	0742x	..	1027x	..	..	1147x	..	1412x	..	1535x	..	1707x	..	..	1830x	..	1830x	..	2102x	..	..	2224x	..	..
22½	Tal-y-Cafn ....d	0747x	....	1032x	....	....	1152x	....	1417x	....	1540x	....	1712x	....	....	1835x	....	1835x	....	2107x	....	....	2229x	....	....
26	Glan Conwy ....d	0753x	..	1038x	..	..	1158x	..	1423x	..	1546x	..	1718x	..	..	1841x	..	1841x	..	2113x	..	..	2235x	..	..
20	**Llandudno Jn** ....a	0757	....	1042	....	....	1202	....	1431	....	1550	....	1726			1845		1845		2117			2239	....	....
—	83 d	0813	..	1047	..	..	1209	..	1433	..	1552	..	1728	..	..	1905	..	1909	..	2119	..	..	2241	..	..
29½	Deganwy ....83 d	0816	....	1050	....	....	1212	....	1436	....	1555	....	1731	....	....	1908	....	1912	....	2122	....	....	2244	....	....
31	**Llandudno** ....83 a	0821	..	1055	..	..	1217	..	1441	..	1600	..	1736	..	..	1913	..	1917	..	2127	..	..	2249	..	..

A 26 May to 8 September
C 28 May to 14 September
D Mondays to Fridays 28 May to 14 September, and Saturdays 26 May to 8 September

b Until 3 November and from 29 March
c 21 July to 25 August
e Mondays to Saturdays Until 3 November and From 29 March
f Mondays to Fridays 28 May to 14 September and Saturdays 21 July to 25 August
g Arr. 1404
h Until 3 November and from 30 March
j Until 2 November and from 29 March
k Mondays to Fridays 28 May to 1 June and 16 July to 31 August Barmouth dep 1145, Harlech dep 1208

n Mondays to Thursdays 28 to 31 May and 16 July to 30 August
p Until 1 June and 16 July to 31 August
q Mondays to Fridays 28 May to 14 September and Saturdays 21 July to 25 August. Mondays to Fridays until 25 May and from 14 September to 2 November and from 29 March and Saturdays until 14 July and from 1 September until 3 November and from 30 March arr 1429
r Mondays to Fridays until 25 May and from 14 September to 2 November and from 29 March and Saturdays until 14 July and from 1 September until 3 November and from 30 March arr 1444

NORTH WALES RADIO LAND CRUISE

by train specially equipped for actual radio reception and descriptive commentary on features of interest en route

A CIRCULAR RAIL TOUR OF OVER 150 MILES EMBRACING SOME OF THE FINEST INLAND AND COASTAL SCENERY IN BRITAIN

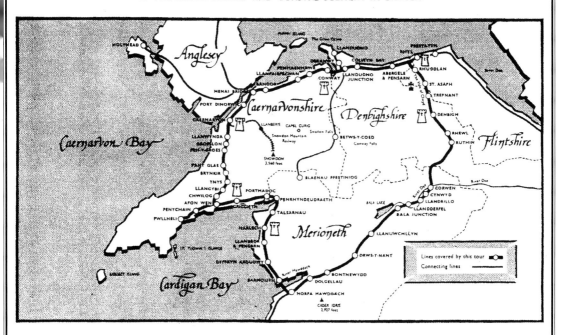

TUESDAYS and THURSDAYS

27th June to 20th July, 1961
(INCLUSIVE)

ALSO

MONDAYS to FRIDAYS

24th July to 8th September, 1961
(INCLUSIVE)

FARE	TIME OF DEPARTURE	FROM	ARRIVAL ON RETURN
s. d.	a.m.		p.m.
	10.10	PWLLHELI	5.28B
	10.18	PENYCHAIN	5.13B
	10.33	CRICCIETH	5.14
	10.43	PORTMADOC	5.23
	10.50	PENRHYNDEUDRAETH	5.34
	10.55	TALSARNAU	5.42
20/-	11. 0	HARLECH	5.46
	11. 6	LLANBEDR & PENSARN	5.58
FROM EACH	11.12	DYFFRYN ARDUDWY	6. 0
STATION	11.15	TALYBONT HALT	6. 3
	11.25	BARMOUTH	6.10
	11.45	PENMAENPOOL	7.36C
	11.50	DOLGELLAU	7.41C
	11.25A	BALA	8.42D
	p.m.		
	12.50	CORWEN	9. 2C

1.58 p.m. arrive **RHYL** depart 3.30 p.m.

A—Change at Bala Junction and Corwen. B—Change at Afon Wen
C—Change at Barmouth. D—Change at Barmouth and Bala Junction
Children under Three years of age, Free ; Three and under Fourteen years of age, Half Fare

Light meals and refreshments may be obtained from the **Cafeteria Car** on the train

BR. 35021

BARMOUTH

II.   The 1913 survey includes both signal boxes (S.B.) and the weighing machine (W.M.). Much of the beach was later used for other purposes.

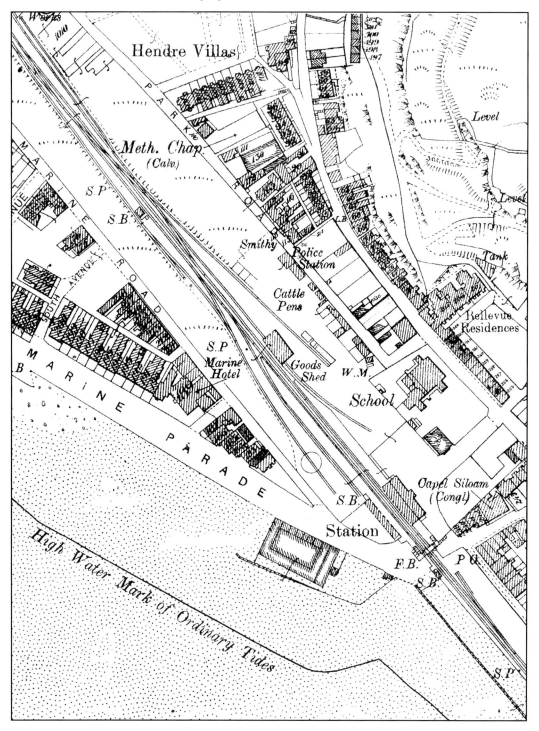

1.   One of the earliest photographs of the station includes the original footbridge, together with 0-4-2 no. 7 *Llanerchydol*, which was built in 1860 by Sharp Stewart. (P.Q.Treloar coll.)

2.   At the north end of the station on 1st June 1932 is GWR 2-4-0 no. 3207 with the 12.9pm to Pwllheli. On the left is a former CR observation car. There was a staff of around 20 in the 1930s. (H.C.Casserley)

3.	A southward view from the 1930s → 4.	Looking north in around 1950, we can see includes more of the bay platform and the down part of the up bay, plus South Box. This had 27 shelter still devoid of a canopy. The gas for the levers after 1924 and was in use from 31st August lamps was supplied by the local gasworks, which 1890 until 22nd October 1988. It was later moved had a siding north of the station. (Stations UK) to the Llangollen Railway. (P.J.Kelley)

5.	The 5.55pm to Pwllheli was recorded on 13th August 1953, the locomotive being "Dukedog" 4-4-0 no. 9018. The full length of the platform was only used during the brief holiday season. (R.M.Casserley)

6.　　　The 1890 North Box had 24 levers until 1924 and 36 thereafter; it closed on 29th September 1974, after goods traffic had ceased. Shunting on 3rd July 1961 is 0-6-0 no. 2251. (L.W.Rowe)

Other views can be found in *Machynlleth to Barmouth*.

7.   The carriage sidings are well filled as 0-6-0 no. 3204 runs south with the breakdown train on 13th August 1962. The hut was for the permanent way trolley. (R.A.Lumber/D.H.Mitchell coll.)

8.   A northward panorama in July 1969 features the footbridge from which the previous two photographs were taken. The trackwork was greatly simplified in 1974. The bridge is officially Hepworth Foot Viaduct and measures 86yds in length. (C.L.Caddy)

9.	The north elevation was photographed in 1977. Following privatisation almost 20 years later, the booking office was closed and a Tourist Information Centre was established therein. It continued to offer railway tickets. (D.A.Thompson)

10.	The narrow width of the town is evident as trains stand in both platforms on 22nd June 1981. The resident population had remained steady: 2214 in 1901 and 2200 in 1961. The through platforms could take ten coaches each. The DMU is class 101. (T.Heavyside)

11.   Nos 31146 and 31166 worked the 09.25 Birmingham New Street to Pwllheli service on 8th August 1992. The siding had earlier continued to the gasworks. The station footbridge had long gone. (P.G.Barnes)

12.   The sole remaining siding is behind no. 76079 as it runs round its tourist train from Machynlleth on 27th August 2006. The siding was in use between at least 1910 and 1963, around 1500 tons of coal running over it to the gasworks in 1938. (M.Turvey)

LLANABER

III.   The 1953 map at 1ins to 1 mile features Barmouth and Barmouth Junction, with the Dolgelley line on the right. The coast route and the A496 are squeezed between the mountains and the beach.

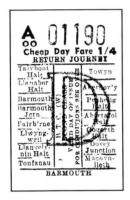

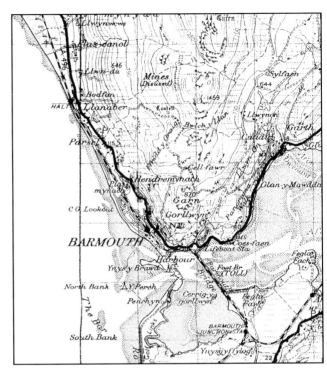

13.   A 1968 photograph includes natural features: the beach thrown onto the track and the steep hillside which gave economy in footbridge construction, with steps on one side only. The halt opened in July 1914. (C.L.Caddy)

14.   The term "Halt" was dropped in 1968 and a class 156 DMU is pictured in 1995. The sea wall had been reinforced further since the previous photograph. The number of residents locally dropped from 702 in 1901 to 340 in 1961. (P.Jones)

Barmouth	1923	1929	1930	1933
Passenger tickets issued	84751	66761	63278	51740
Season tickets issued	149	100	327	832
Parcels forwarded	37468	35187	35111	36850
General goods forwarded (tons)	523	398	435	620
Coal and coke received (tons)	3465	3723	3155	2940
Other minerals received (tons)	1913	917	1291	1205
General goods received (tons)	3498	3155	5098	2730
Trucks of livestock handled	125	124	115	112

1444

2nd - CHARTER CONTROL
Festiniog Railway Society Ltd.
29th APRIL, 1972
London (Euston) Watford Junction
Rugby Birmingham or Wolverhampton
TO
MINFFORDD AND BACK
Coach letter... Seat No...1... Back/Facing
(M) For conditions see over

0299

TALYBONT

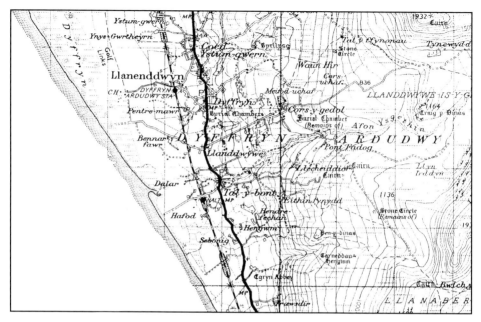

IV.   A continuation of the last map reveals that the railway builders had an easier task with the need for only a few cuttings on the coastal plain.

15.   The halt opened in July 1914 and was the subject for a postcard in the 1930s, "Wish you were here". (Lens of Sutton coll.)

16.   Platform lengthening had taken place by 1964, but the earlier shelter remained. There was easy access to the beach. (Stations UK)

17.   A class 103 DMU forms the 10.25 from Barmouth and was recorded on 28th September 1971, when the sign was devoid of "Halt". It had been lost in 1968. (C.L.Caddy)

DYFFRYN ARDUDWY

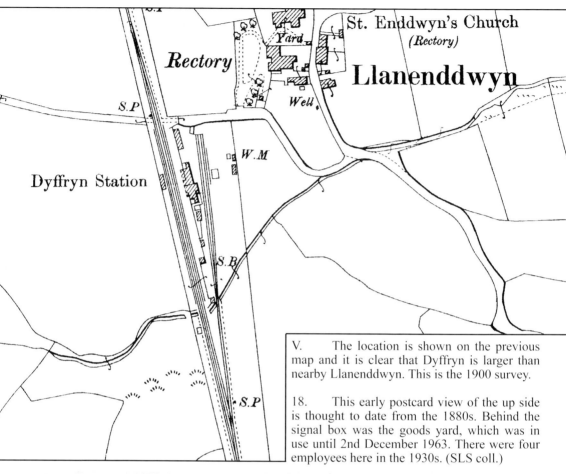

Rectory

Yard

St. Enddwyn's Church
(Rectory)

Llanenddwyn

S.P

W.M

Dyffryn Station

S.B

S.P

V.   The location is shown on the previous map and it is clear that Dyffryn is larger than nearby Llanenddwyn. This is the 1900 survey.

18.   This early postcard view of the up side is thought to date from the 1880s. Behind the signal box was the goods yard, which was in use until 2nd December 1963. There were four employees here in the 1930s. (SLS coll.)

19.　　Sharp Stewart built no. 18 *Orleton* for the CR in 1875. It was an 0-6-0 and lasted until 1919. The platforms would take five coaches each. (P.Q.Treloar coll.)

20.　　The name was as shown from 1924 until 1948, presumably to encourage tourism, but not to please the Welsh. The GWR introduced camp coaches in 1934, although other railways used the term "camping". (GWR)

21.   No. 78002 arrives with a stopping train to Pwllheli in July 1957. The signal box had 13 levers and was in use between about 1891 and 1970. (J.W.T.House/C.L.Caddy coll.)

22.   The down platform was retained, as it was on the straight alignment. A class 158 is departing south in July 2007, when staff was still provided for the little used level crossing, behind the camera. (P.Jones)

LLANBEDR

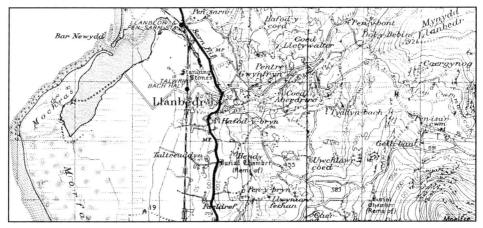

VI.   Opened as Talwrn Bach Halt on 9th July 1923, this stop was closer to Llanbedr than the station then carrying its name. Both are shown on the 1953 edition at 1ins to 1 mile.

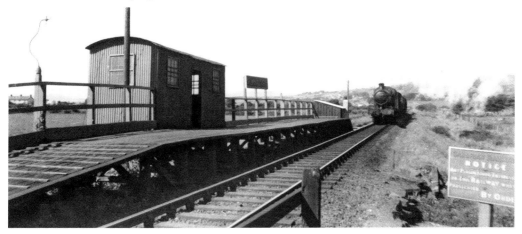

23.   A northward panorama in 1954 includes a train from Pwllheli. "Halt" was dropped in 1968 and the name was changed to Llanbedr in 1978. (Stations UK)

24.   The RAF built an airfield west of the line in 1941, but it was not marked on the map for security reasons. It was later used for guided missiles and pilotless aircraft and was bought by the Welsh Assembly Government in 2002, with the intention of letting a lease to an airport operator. The 17.07 Pwllheli to Machynlleth brakes on 6th October 1972, as dusk descends. (C.L.Caddy)

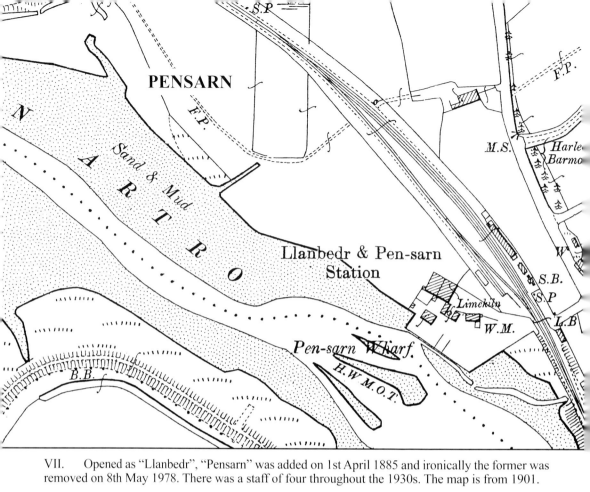

PENSARN

N

A R T R O

Sand & Mud

Sand & Mud

F.P.

Llanbedr & Pen-sarn
Station

Pen-sarn Wharf.

H.W.M.O.T.

B.B.

Limekiln

W.M.

M.S.

Harle
Barmo

S.B.

S.P

L.B

F.P.

VII.   Opened as "Llanbedr", "Pensarn" was added on 1st April 1885 and ironically the former was removed on 8th May 1978. There was a staff of four throughout the 1930s. The map is from 1901.

25.   The south end of the loop was recorded on 21st August 1952. Both lines were signalled for bidirectional running, as there was only one platform. It can take seven coaches.
(H.F.Wheeller/R.S.Carpenter coll.)

26.   No. 9016 is approaching the platform from the south on the same day, having crossed the 104yd-long bridge over the Afon Artro, which is in the background. The locomotive is hauling an inspection saloon. (H.F.Wheeller/R.S.Carpenter coll.)

27.   No. 9018 heads the 5.55pm from Barmouth on 13th August 1953 and passes the goods yard, which closed on 4th May 1964. The leading coaches carry carriage roof boards. (R.M.Casserley)

28.   A July 1964 panorama includes the 34-lever signal box, which was in use from 13th June 1937 until 28th December 1969, when the loop was abandoned. Staffing ceased on 6th May 1968. (C.L.Caddy)

→ 29. The timber bridge was recorded on 3rd May 1983, as the 14.28 from Dovey Junction was crossing it. The formation was class 101 DMUs. The summit of Moelfre is in the background. (P.Johnson)

→   30. The road in the foreground once served a small wharf, as well as the goods yard. The minimal accommodation is seen in May 2007, when only pedestrians crossed the line regularly. (C.L.Caddy)

Dyffryn-on-Sea	1923	1929	1930	1933
Passenger tickets issued	21400	14897	15494	11883
Season tickets issued	94	106	119	113
Parcels forwarded	4208	4091	5016	5211
General goods forwarded (tons)	55	79	37	53
Coal and coke received (tons)	715	781	1029	728
Other minerals received (tons)	388	504	799	277
General goods received (tons)	745	900	879	903
Trucks of livestock handled	93	202	189	169

Llanbedr and Pensarn	1923	1929	1930	1933
Passenger tickets issued	13821	8200	6423	6030
Season tickets issued	79	47	57	90
Parcels forwarded	3840	3321	3182	3342
General goods forwarded (tons)	301	127	1229	86
Coal and coke received (tons)	373	511	264	332
Other minerals received (tons)	364	613	500	743
General goods received (tons)	1230	1177	1253	803
Trucks of livestock handled	254	199	179	117

LLANDANWG

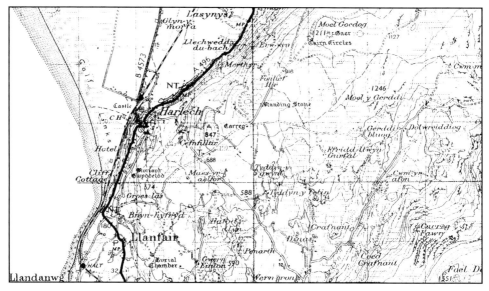

VIII.   The relationship of the halt (lower left) to Harlech and the coast is shown on this 1953 survey at 1ins to 1 mile. The halt opened on 8th November 1929.

31.   No. 46424 is hauling the "Coronation Land Cruise" southwards on 28th July 1953 and is turning inland. This train ran on Tuesdays, Wednesdays and Thursdays that Summer from Llandudno. It went via Rhyl, Corwen, Dolgelley, Afon Wen and Bangor, then back along the North Coast. In subsequent years it ran as the "Radio Land Cruise" from Pwllheli in the opposite direction, five days per week at its peak popularity.
(H.F.Wheeller/R.S.Carpenter coll.)

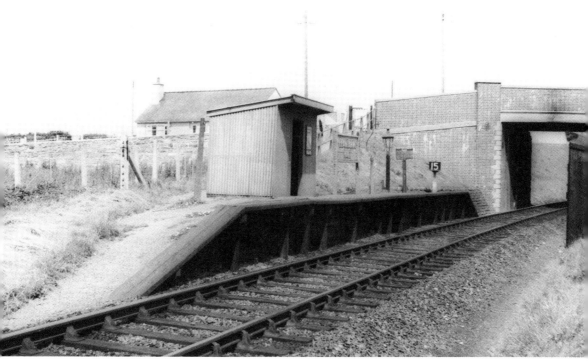

32. The facilities were pictured on 13th July 1964 and the suffix "Halt" was discontinued in 1968. The platform officially accommodates 1½ coaches. (C.L.Caddy)

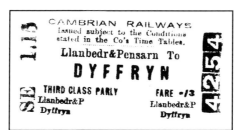

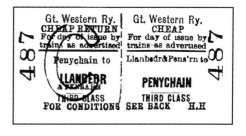

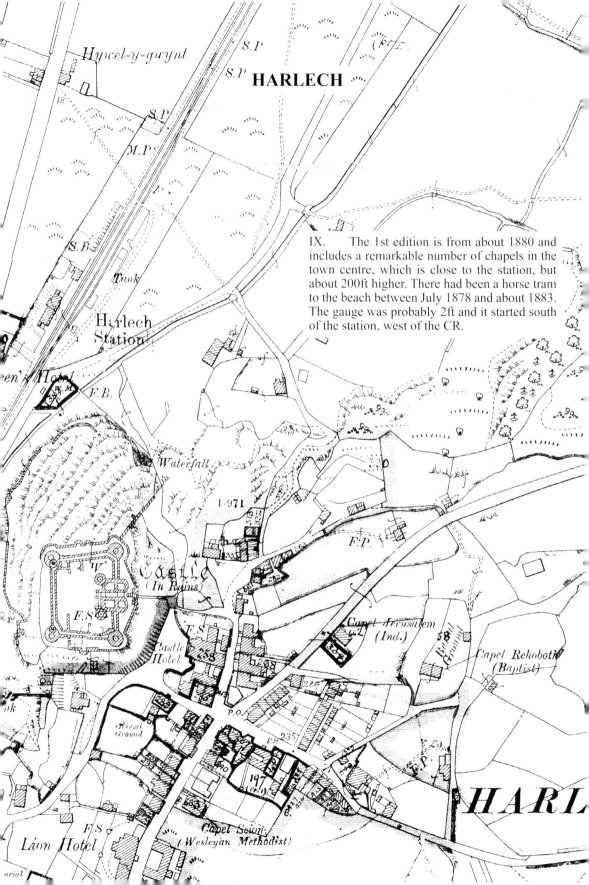

HARLECH

Hyncel-y-gwynt

S.P

S.P

S.P

M.P

S.B

Tank

Harlech
Station

en's Hotel

W.M

F.B.

Waterfall

1.971

Castle
(In Ruins)

W

F.S

F.S

Castle
Hotel

Capel Jerusalem
(Ind.)

Capel Rehoboth
(Baptist)

P.O.

P.H.

Burial
Ground

197
(Pro)

HARL

F.S

Lion Hotel

Capel Seion
(Wesleyan Methodist)

IX.   The 1st edition is from about 1880 and includes a remarkable number of chapels in the town centre, which is close to the station, but about 200ft higher. There had been a horse tram to the beach between July 1878 and about 1883. The gauge was probably 2ft and it started south of the station, west of the CR.

33.   The impressive architecture of the castle and the elegant style of the Sharp Stewart 4-4-0 no. 50 were recorded on 15th November 1911. The locomotive was in use from 1891 to 1925 and is coupled to a horse box and carriage truck forming part of the 2.43pm from Pwllheli. (P.Q.Treloar coll.)

34.   No details are available for this view, which is probably from the 1930s. There were five employees in that decade. The line on the right ran to the goods siding, which also had a connection at its far end. (Stations UK)

35.   A similar perspective on 17th October 1962 includes the then recent footbridge. Many schoolchildren use this station and at a time when trains are passing one another, hence the improved safety provision. The goods yard closed on 2nd November 1964. (P.J.Kelley coll.)

36.   Taken moments later, this view includes the second stage of the lamp changing procedure, as the distant arm receives attention. The bay window enabled the station master to survey his territory from behind net curtains. (P.J.Kelley coll.)

37.   The panorama from the castle on 31st October 1975 includes the 1924 signal box, which had 29 levers and lasted until 23rd October 1988. The down platform takes ten coaches and the up side nine. (M.Farr)

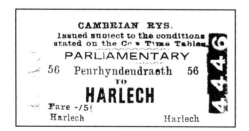

38.   Regional Railways' DMU no. 153356 forms the 17.06 Machynlleth to Pwllheli on 25th
June 1996 and passes over the site of the level crossing seen earlier. The next one south is in the
background and the road on the left of picture 36 provides the link. (M.J.Stretton)

Harlech	1923	1929	1930	1933
Passenger tickets issued	23114	16066	15855	18418
Season tickets issued	72	106	90	148
Parcels forwarded	7313	8420	8870	9687
General goods forwarded (tons)	123	83	125	76
Coal and coke received (tons)	356	844	959	552
Other minerals received (tons)	2922	751	562	1088
General goods received (tons)	928	569	632	528
Trucks of livestock handled	251	207	244	209

39.   No. 76079 runs south with the "Cambrian Coast Express" destined for Machynlleth on 25th
August 2005. West Coast Railways operated this service, which called only at the main towns and
junctions. (M.Turvey)

TYGWYN

X.   North of Harlech, the line continues straight and level on the coastal plain, which has sand
dunes close to the foreshore.

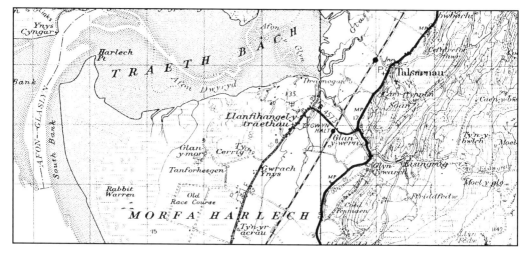

40.   The halt came into use on 11th July 1927 and is seen on 25th May 1964, complete with a lantern for an oil lamp. An automatic barrier removed the need for gate staff around 1980. (C.L.Caddy)

41.   The one-coach platform and old shelter remained unchanged when the 16.38 Machynlleth to Pwllheli was recorded passing on 24th June 1986. The class 150 units were unpopular, largely due to their high noise level. (C.L.Caddy)

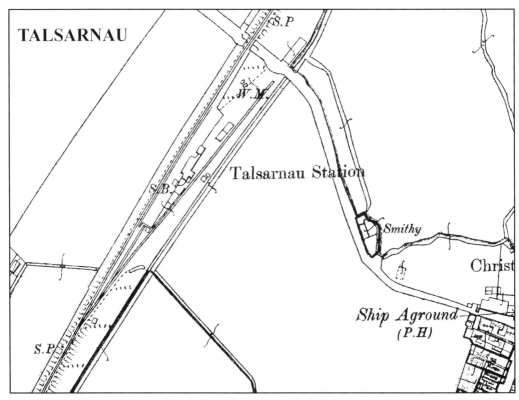

TALSARNAU

S.P

W.M.

Talsarnau Station

S.B.

Smithy

Christ

Ship Aground
(P.H)

S.P.

XI.   The 1901 survey shows a simple layout, which remained unchanged. W.M. indicates Weighing Machine. There was a staff of four here in the 1930s.

42.   A southward panorama in 1964 has the parcels shed nearest, with the unroofed facilities for gentlemen beyond. The goods yard closed that year, on 4th May. The platform length is four coaches. (C.L.Caddy)

43.　　This is a 1968 view; staffing ceased that year, on 6th May and the 11-lever signal box closed that day. The crossing in the distance became "user-worked". (R.F.Roberts/SLS coll.)

Gt. Western Ry.	Gt. Western Ry
Talsarnau	Talsarnau
TO	
DYFFRYN-ARDUDWY	
THIRD CLASS	
1/11 Z　Fare　1/11 Z	
Dyffryn Ardudwy	Dyffryn Ardudwy
FOR CONDITIONS SEE BACK　(W.L	

8259　　8259

Talsarnau	1923	1929	1930	1933
Passenger tickets issued	13674	10112	10751	10120
Season tickets issued	73	52	60	58
Parcels forwarded	2408	2765	2671	2901
General goods forwarded (tons)	133	41	44	45
Coal and coke received (tons)	243	247	201	137
Other minerals received (tons)	153	392	318	639
General goods received (tons)	442	348	409	413
Trucks of livestock handled	86	73	49	34

LLANDECWYN

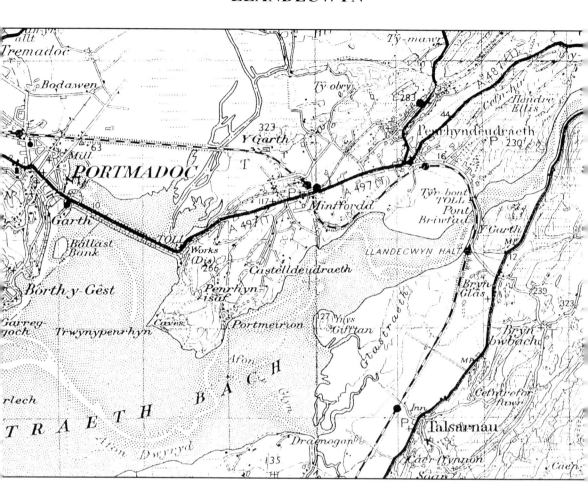

← XII. Opened on 11th November 1935, the halt is on the south bank of the Afon Dwyryd down which small boats sailed with slates until the opening of the Festiniog Railway (top) in 1836. The 1953 map is scaled at 1½ ins to 1 mile.

← 44. The simple structure was photographed in 1964 with water on the right and marshland on the left. The oil lamp was an optional extra, but the step for guards to reach the hook was a fixture. (Stations UK)

45.   No. 43151 pauses on 11th July 1966 with an inspecton saloon; the nearest dwellings are on the left. The suffix "Halt" was dropped in 1968. (M.J.Stretton coll.)

2nd-SINGLE SINGLE-2nd

Penrhyndeudraeth to

Penrhyndeudraeth   Penrhyndendraeth
Tygwyn Halt   Tygwyn Halt

TYGWYN HALT

(W)   8d.   Fare   8d.   (W)

For conditions see over For conditions see over

2nd-SINGLE   SINGLE-2nd

Penrhyndeudraeth to

Penrhyndeudraeth   Penrhyndeudraeth
Llandecwyn Halt   Llandecwyn Halt

LLANDECWYN HALT

(M)   0/4   Fare   0/4   (M)
For conditions see over   For conditions see over

46. Traeth Bach Viaduct is 148yds in length and is seen on 22nd June 1981 as the 10.30 Pwllheli to Shrewsbury class 101 DMU runs towards us. The toll road is railway property and in the background is Cookes Explosives Works. (T.Heavyside)

47. The Briwet Bridge is the alternative name for the wooden structure, which is viewed from the down "Cambrian Coast Express" from Machynlleth on 3rd August 2007. An industrial estate occupies the former Cookes' site. (V.Mitchell)

Penrhyndeudraeth	1923	1929	1930	1933
Passenger tickets issued	23614	16456	13785	13536
Season tickets issued	27	60	99	112
Parcels forwarded	7225	8558	8473	9191
General goods forwarded (tons)	411	676	534	655
Coal and coke received (tons)	310	1532	1158	914
Other minerals received (tons)	911	895	769	284
General goods received (tons)	1463	2275	2107	2237
Trucks of livestock handled	97	79	79	44

PENRHYNDEUDRAETH

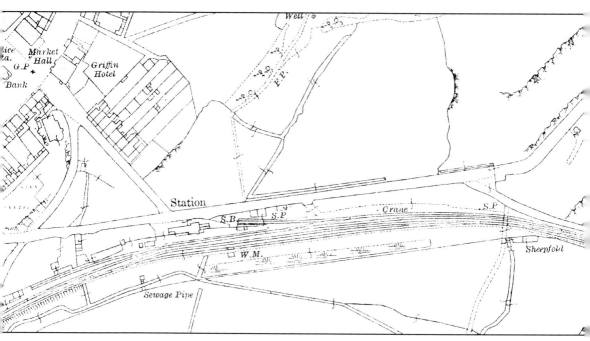

XIII.   The 1901 survey includes a weighing machine, which was for railway wagons only. Top left is the centre of the town, which had a population of a little over 2000 for the first half of the 20th century.

48.   A view west in about 1939 includes the weigh house on the left and the single line tablet catcher on the right. As at Caersws and Llanbedr & Pensarn, the CR economised by not providing a platform on the passing loop. (Stations UK)

49.   Seen on the same occasion is no. 2490, one of the GWR's 2301 class 0-6-0s, introduced in 1883. The tanker is of the type used for tar and other chemicals. There were six men employed here in the 1930s. (Stations UK)

50.   The dock siding had cattle pens nearby. The 10.25am Pwllheli to Dovey Junction, headed by nos. 2233 and 5510, is viewed from the 6.55am from Wrexham which is in the loop on 20th June 1959. (J.Langford)

51.　　Seen in August 1961 is 2-6-0 no. 75020 and the short coal siding. In the background is the steep gradient of 1 in 65 over the headland. On the right is the iron lamp room. (D.K.Jones coll.)

52.　　Most buildings in the background of this 1964 view were associated with industrial explosives, some of which were used in local quarries, but most of which were despatched in steel vans of the type seen. The crane (centre) was listed as being of 3-ton capacity. (C.L.Caddy)

53.   The platform would take only three coaches. Entering it on 3rd July 1969 is the 10.25 Barmouth to Pwllheli, class 101 DMU. The signal box had an 18 lever frame, which was in use from 10th August 1891 to 9th December 1973, when the sidings and loops were abandoned. Explosives were subsequently taken by road to Blaenau Ffestiniog for forwarding by rail. (C.L.Caddy)

54.   The 06.41 from Machynlleth arrives on 9th May 1995. The station buildings are fenced off, having been sold in 1979 for residential purposes. (M.J.Stretton)

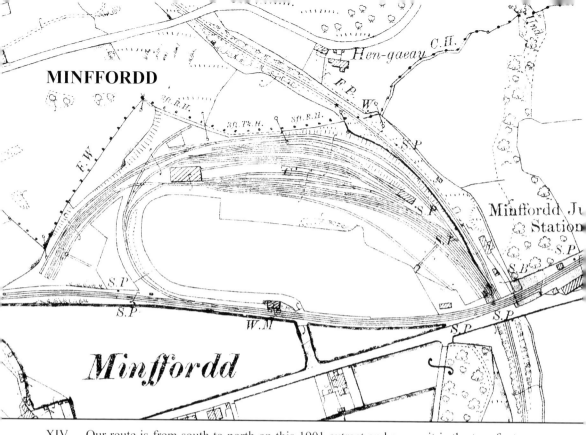

MINFFORDD

Minffordd

XIV. Our route is from south to north on this 1901 extract and across it is the two-foot gauge Festiniog Railway. The exchange sidings and stations came into use on 1st August 1872. Vast quantities of slate were transferred from the FR to the CR and much coal moved in the other direction, along with local goods.

55. The FR station roofs are in the left background and two of its tracks, together with the main road, are on the bridge in this late 1930s view. The path to the FR and the road is at the far end of the building. The FR passenger service was withdrawn in September 1939 and goods traffic ceased in August 1946. (Stations UK)

56.　　Two photographs from 16th September 1949 include FR wagons still loaded with slates. The goods shed on the left contained tracks of both gauges. The lorry on the right brought slates from the quarries and also your author (VM) on his first visit in 1951. (R.S.Carpenter coll.)

57.　　Moving to the north of the goods shed the photographer recorded the overgrown sunken sidings, which had been used for the transfer of coal to the FR. The station buildings of both lines are in the background, as is part of the crane which was rated at 2½ tons. (R.S.Carpenter coll.)

58.   The south end of the six-coach platform was photographed in 1956, the year in which the revived FR opened between Portmadoc and Minffordd. The next picture is the driver's view. (Ted Hancock Books)

59.   This is the summit of the line over the headland between the valleys of the Dwyryd and the Glaslyn. There were two men here in the 1930s, but only one in the final years of staffing, which ceased on 19th October 1964. (M.J.Stretton coll.)

60.   There were no signals, as the box was not a block post. It had 19 levers and was in use from 1893 until 23rd March 1973, when the line to the left closed. Public goods traffic had ceased on 7th February 1966. Recorded on 27th June 1957 is ex-GWR 2-6-2T no. 4599, with a local train. (P.Q.Treloar)

61.   Royal train admirers gathered on 9th August 1963 as no. 7819 *Hinton Manor* piloted no. 7822 *Foxcote Manor*. Note the special headcode. The vertical white lines on the wagons indicated shock resistant bodies required for slates. (D.Rouse/M.J.Stretton coll.)

Miles		BHX				C SX			C SX			C SX	A SO		D
—	Barmouth ....76 d		0800n		0817	1030k	1145p	1333b		1521	1500		1805n			
—	Pwllheli ....76 d					1015b	1215	1215b		1500			1645n			
—	Harlech ....76 d				0847	1100k	1208p	1356b		1549			1832n			
—	Porthmadog Harbour....510 d		0840n		0950	1220b	1310	1455b		1635	1635c		1900n			
—	Minffordd ....510, 76 d		0849n		0959	1229b	1319	1504b		1644	1644c		1900n			
0	**Blaenau Ffestiniog** ....d	0700	0945		1105	1330	1450	1625		1748	1748	2020			2142
5	Roman Bridge ....d	0711x	0956x		1116x	1341x	1501x	1636x		1759x	1759x	2031x			2153x
6½	Dolwyddelan ....d	0715x	1000x		1120x	1345x	1505x	1640x		1803x	1803x	2035x			2157x
8½	Pont-y-Pant ....d	0719x	1004x		1124x	1349x	1509x	1644x		1807x	1807x	2039x			2201x
12½	Betws-y-Coed ....d	0728	1013		1133	1358	1518	1653		1816	1816	2048			2210
16½	Llanrwst ....d	0735	1020		1140	1405	1525	1700		1825	1825	2055			2217
19½	Dolgarrog ....d	0742x	1027x		1147x	1412x	1535x	1707x		1830x	1829x	2102x			2224x
22½	Tal-y-Cafn ....d	0747x	1032x		1152x	1417x	1540x	1712x		1835x	1835x	2107x			2229x
26	Glan Conwy ....d	0753x	1038x		1158x	1423x	1546x	1718x		1841x	1841x	2113x			2235x
28	Llandudno Jn ....a	0757	1042		1202	1431	1550	1726		1845	1845	2117			2239
		0813	1047		1209	1433	1552	1728		1905	1909	2119			2241
29½	Deganwy ....83 d	0816	1050		1212	1436	1555	1731		1908	1913	2122			2244
31	Llandudno ....83 a	0821	1055		1217	1441	1600	1736		1913	1917	2127			2249

A 26 May to 8 September
C 28 May to 14 September
D Mondays to Fridays 28 May to 14 September, and Saturdays 26 May to 8 September

b Until 3 November and from 29 March
c 21 July to 25 August
e Mondays to Saturdays Until 3 November and From 29 March
f Mondays to Fridays 28 May to 14 September and Saturdays 21 July to 25 August
g Arr. 1404
h Until 3 November and from 30 March
j Until 2 November and from 29 March
k Mondays to Fridays 28 May to 1 June and 16 July to 31 August Barmouth dep 1145, Harlech dep 1208

n Mondays to Thursdays 28 to 31 May and 16 July to 30 August
p Until 1 June and 16 July to 31 August
q Mondays to Fridays 28 May to 14 September and Saturdays 21 July to 25 August. Mondays to Fridays until 25 May and from 14 September to 2 November and from 29 March and Saturdays until 14 July and from 1 September until 3 November and from 30 March arr 1429
r Mondays to Fridays until 25 May and from 14 September to 2 November and from 29 March and Saturdays until 14 July and from 1 September until 3 November and from 30 March arr 1444

The BR timetable for the Summer of 1984 showed the connections between the Cambrian Coast and the North Coast via the recently fully restored FR.

62.   A low maintenance shelter had arrived by 3rd May 1967, when no. D5084 was shunting. It had left its train on the 1 in 50 incline up from the floor of the Glaslyn Estuary. Slates are stacked on the edge of the Maenofferen Wharf awaiting loading. Wagon load traffic continued until 30th May 1972. (R.F.Roberts/SLS coll.)

63.　　It is July 1975 and *Blanche* is on the bridge, as the signal box awaits demolition. The FR took over local BR ticket sales in 1965 and from this evolved Ffestiniog Travel, now an international business operating from modern offices about 300yds to the south of the station. (M.Farr)

Minffordd	1923	1929	1930	1933
Passenger tickets issued	14694	4245	4178	3455
Season tickets issued	19	10	14	17
Parcels forwarded	1012	897	1030	1107
Minerals forwarded (tons)	108905	73283	71169	43793
General goods forwarded (tons)	77	164	167	112
Coal and coke received (tons)	1438	906	389	32
Other minerals received (tons)	2286	1510	1482	575
General goods received (tons)	497	176	227	100
Trucks of livestock handled	-	-	-	-

Other albums to feature this unique station are:

Branch Lines around Portmadoc 1923-46
Branch Lines around Porthmadog 1954-94
Festiniog 1946-55 - The Pioneers' Stories
Festiniog in the Fifties
Festiniog in the Sixties
Festiniog 50 years of Enterprise
Return to Blaenau 1970-82

64.   The exchange sidings became the FR's permanent way and general storage yard, as seen on 22nd June 1981 as class 101 no. M51176 arrives. Earlier, there had been a siding for the granite quarry in the background, the points being at its west end. (T.Heavyside)

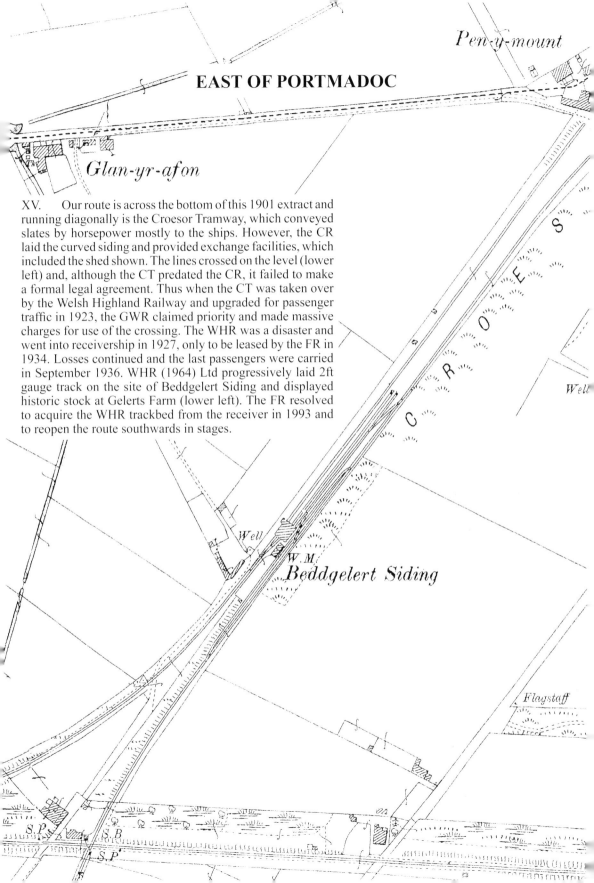

Pen-y-mount

Glan-yr-afon

XV.   Our route is across the bottom of this 1901 extract and running diagonally is the Croesor Tramway, which conveyed slates by horsepower mostly to the ships. However, the CR laid the curved siding and provided exchange facilities, which included the shed shown. The lines crossed on the level (lower left) and, although the CT predated the CR, it failed to make a formal legal agreement. Thus when the CT was taken over by the Welsh Highland Railway and upgraded for passenger traffic in 1923, the GWR claimed priority and made massive charges for use of the crossing. The WHR was a disaster and went into receivership in 1927, only to be leased by the FR in 1934. Losses continued and the last passengers were carried in September 1936. WHR (1964) Ltd progressively laid 2ft gauge track on the site of Beddgelert Siding and displayed historic stock at Gelerts Farm (lower left). The FR resolved to acquire the WHR trackbed from the receiver in 1993 and to reopen the route southwards in stages.

CROESOR

Well

Well

W.M.

Beddgelert Siding

Flagstaff

S.P.

S.B.

S.P.

65.　　The main line is on the left and its station is in the distance. The town had three stations, but only one with a suffix (Harbour). In 2008 your author became editor and publisher of RAIL TIMES for Great Britain and endeavoured to rectify the problem, but to no avail. However, his term "North" for this station was gradually coming into use, but too late for this album. A 1952 Ruston & Hornsby is seen with a WHR(1964) train on 8th September 1984. (T.Heavyside)

Portmadoc	1923	1929	1930	1933
Passenger tickets issued	57235	34127	29833	28619
Season tickets issued	86	9	27	93
Parcels forwarded	27737	25042	26066	29204
Minerals forwarded (tons)	37608	25803	17825	9202
General goods forwarded (tons)	4152	2868	3085	1621
Coal and coke received (tons)	2011	2032	1823	2076
Other minerals received (tons)	1377	1779	1525	1225
General goods received (tons)	6260	7521	7314	4096
Trucks of livestock handled	305	222	294	235

66.   The same station is viewed from the "Cambrian Coast Express" on 3rd August 2007, after total redevelopment. The building contains an excellent shop and splendid buffet. A trip on the train to Pen-y-Mount (top right on the map) included a tour of the extensive museum on the return journey. With its splendid and varied stock collection, it is in effect the Welsh Heritage Railway, a name which would attract more visitors and also end confusion. (V.Mitchell)

67.   The crossing was lifted in 1938 and relaid 70 years later. Seen on 12th March 2009 is the first locomotive to cross it, the FR's *Vale of Ffestiniog*. Signalling was a long way off, both here and along the A487 trunk road over Britannia Bridge, near Harbour station. Part of the Cross Town Rail Link had grooved tram rail made in Austria and was an astonishing part of the £28m project. The end of the new Pullman observation car no. 2100 is included. (R.Dimmick)

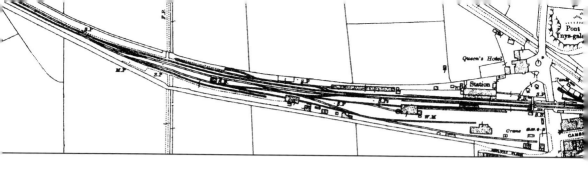

PORTMADOC

XVI.   The 1913 survey at 15ins to 1 mile has the Croesor Tramway from top to bottom. It runs under a shelter attached to the corn mill, over Snowdon Street and then alongside the gasworks, both of which could be served. The FR terminus is lower centre and a triangular junction was laid at the south end of the High Street in 1923 to enable WHR trains to access the FR. The CR purchased land in 1865 on which to lay a siding to the harbour, it being shown by a pair of curved boundary fences on the right. It is not known if a lifting span in Britannia Bridge for ships was planned. The gasworks was in use from 1859 until 1963 and used 1194 tons of coal in 1938.

68.   This southward view in about 1910 is from outside the Queens Hotel and includes the approach to the cattle docks on the left. The level crossing gates are unclear; only their lamps are evident. The isolated coach must be in a shunting manoeuvre, while the crane stands amidst masses of timber on the right. (Welsh Highland Heritage Group)

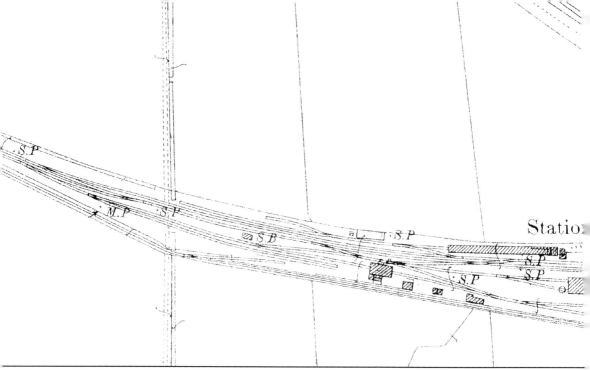

XVII. This 1901 map continues from no. XV and Beddgelert Siding is the upper line on the right. The diagonal lines represent Y Cyt, an early waterway to Tremadoc alongside which ran the Gorseddau Tramway from 1855 to 1867. A small vestige of it is on the previous map, west of the corn mill. The signal box near the bridge was called "Gorsedda Crossing" and its 12-lever frame →

69.   A Pwllheli to Barmouth stopping train waits to leave behind 0-6-0 no. 2468 on 9th August 1935. The building dates from 1873. For many years, coaches for Euston via Bangor started here and joined others from Pwllheli at Afon Wen. (H.F.Wheeller/R.S.Carpenter coll.)

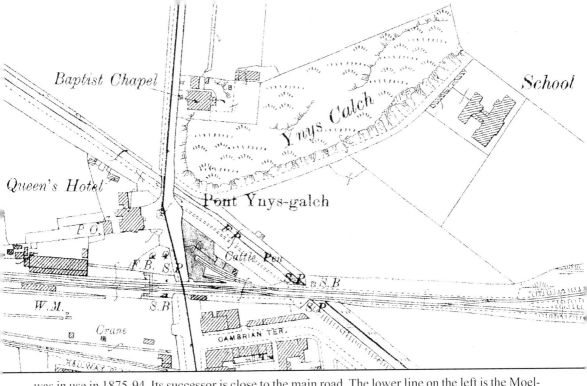

was in use in 1875-94. Its successor is close to the main road. The lower line on the left is the Moel-y-Gest Tramway and is fenced off from the CR, although a short siding from it passes through a gate for exchange traffic. The centre line on the left is a headshunt. The 32-lever West Box (left) closed in 1932.

70.   Another westward view is from the 1930s, when there was a staff of 30-33, this including train crew. On the left is Moel-y-Gest and its granite quarries, but the crane (see map) is just out of view. It was uprated from three to six tons in 1931. (Stations UK)

71.　A 1948 panorama has the down water column and the 1931 goods shed on the left. On the right is the engine shed. Beddgelert siding and some others were lifted in 1973, but one long one was retained and was used by "Cambrian Coast Express" trains terminating here in 2007-08. (R.G.Nelson coll.)

72.　"Dukedog" 4-4-0 no. 9015 runs in with the 8.40am Pwllheli to Machynlleth on 29th June 1957, as the wheel tapper looks on. Suggs Rochester pattern gaslamps are evident, while their Windsor model graces the previous view. (P.Q.Treloar)

73.   Nos 2204 and 78005 were recorded "on shed" on 11th September 1960, when there were 28 crew members listed. Several worked the route to Bangor. The footbridge and loading gauge are not seen in the other photographs. The town had a population of almost 4000 at this period. The engine shed closed in August 1963; it had an allocation of nine engines back in 1947. (R.S.Carpenter)

74.   Known as East Box until 1932, the 1894 structure housed a 38-lever frame thereafter and functioned until 23rd October 1988. The photograph is from 1969 and includes the "cow horn" and net for receiving the single line tablet. (C.L.Caddy)

75.   DMUs were recorded passing on 29th May 1970. The down side structures were all destroyed, but the up building was in use in the 21st century as licensed premises. The water tank had gone. Freight continued until about 1978. (R.Ruffell/M.J.Stretton coll.)

PORTHMADOG

76.   The name of the town was changed in 1974, although the Port had been created by Mr. Madock. He had initiated the construction of The Cob on which the FR was laid. Nos 25037 and 25021 wait with the 13.50 Pwllheli to Paddington return charter. It had a three-hour layover here on 24th August 1986 which was a Sunday. (D.H.Mitchell)

WEST OF PORTMADOC

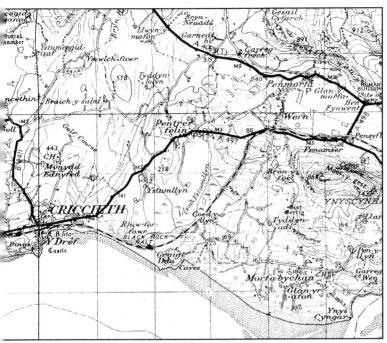

XVIII. The railway and the road are close together for over one mile west of the town and there is a gradient of 1 in 50 to climb over the ridge to reach the coast. This is the 1953 edition at 1ins to 1 mile.

XIX. The 1900 edition includes Wern siding, which was used mainly by Wern Manor, for long the estate of Richard Greaves, a Blaenau Ffestiniog quarry owner. Traffic ceased in 1957. The bridge over the main road is on the right. It became the A497 in 1919. Ballast for the railway was loaded here at one period and there was a 4-ton crane for timber traffic.

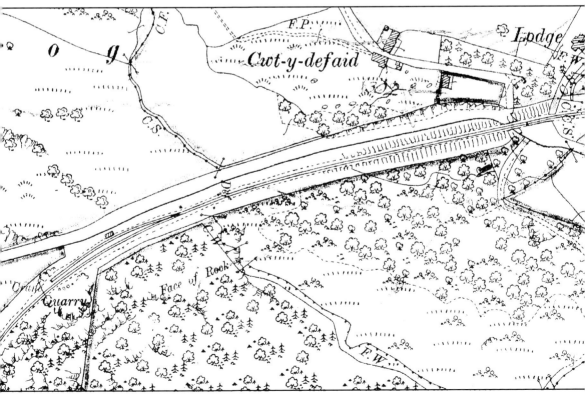

77.   "Dukedog" 4-4-0 no. 9025 works hard on the gradient south of Wern on 15th July 1954.
The descent to the coast was easy, at 1 in 54. (M.J.Stretton coll.)

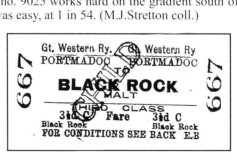

BLACK ROCK

78.   The halt was on the down side and was opened on 9th July 1923, entirely for the benefit of visitors to the beach. It was a request stop. It ceased to be called a halt in 1968. (Lens of Sutton coll.)

79.   The footpath to the sands is evident in this eastward view of Moel-y-Gest from July 1969, by which time a modern sign had arrived, but the hut had gone. The structure became unsafe and was not used after 13th August 1976. (C.L.Caddy)

EAST OF CRICCIETH

80.   There were two manned crossings on the approach to the station; this is the second and was called Maes Crossing. It is seen in June 1970. (C.L.Caddy)

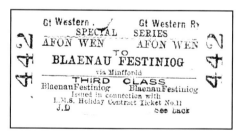

Criccieth	1923	1929	1930	1933
Passenger tickets issued	44181	24131	21273	21408
Season tickets issued	209	141	183	284
Parcels forwarded	14444	14504	13588	15802
General goods forwarded (tons)	209	167	224	173
Coal and coke received (tons)	373	423	388	335
Other minerals received (tons)	1048	1158	688	647
General goods received (tons)	1499	1500	1404	1465
Trucks of livestock handled	290	223	231	134

CRICCIETH

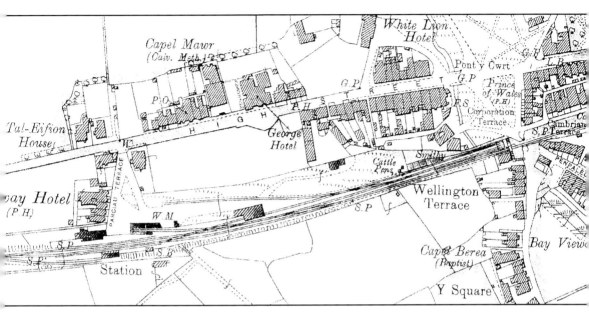

XX.   The 1900 edition is at 20ins to 1 mile. The number of residents was 1406 in 1901 and 1580 in 1961.

81.   In this undated postcard we look east and find a short bay platform on the down side and an iron lamp room on the up side. The main buildings dated from 1873, as at Portmadoc. (SLS coll.)

82.   A 1952 panorama confirms the remarkably rural location of the station at that time. There is a coach in the bay and a class 2 2-6-0 arriving with freight. (J.Moss/R.S.Carpenter coll.)

83.   Standard class 4 4-6-0 no. 75020 heads the 11.30am Pwllheli to Wrexham train on 20th June 1959. Goods traffic continued until 5th October 1964. The shed contained a one-ton hand crane. (J.Langford)

84.   No. 46509 waits with the 12.45pm Pwllheli to Wrexham on 8th August 1964, while no. 82009 runs in with the 7.50am Birkenhead to Pwllheli. In the 1930s, there were eight to ten men employed here. The line in the foreground ran to the loading dock. (D.A.Johnson)

85.   With a fine clear view for passengers, class 108 DMU pulls into the six-car up platform on 12th May 1966, working the 10.20 Pwllheli to Dovey Junction. Staffing ceased on 6th May 1968. (R.F.Roberts/SLS coll.)

86. A class 103 forms the 06.50 Machynlleth to Pwllheli and arrives on 23rd June 1981. The 1892 signal box had 22 levers and was taken out of use on 16th October 1977, when the loop was abandoned. (T.Heavyside)

87. Nos 37431 and 37181 hauled the 07.30 from Euston on the Welsh part of the journey on 20th September 1986. The return of locomotives after years of despair was most welcome; sadly it was to be the last year of a London service. (B.Robbins)

AFON WEN

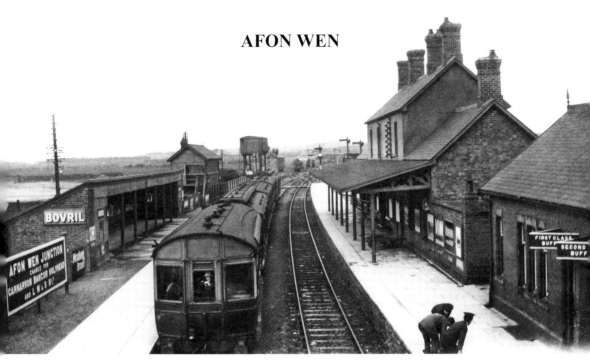

88.   The locomotive in the distance is near the end of the siding on the left of the map, while on the right is a choice of buffets. The coach in the foreground is an observation car and carries a roof board. (R.M.Casserley coll.)

89.   Cars of the 1930s are evident in this westward panorama, which includes Butlins Holiday Camp in the left background. The building includes four cottages for railwaymen. (M.J.Stretton coll.)

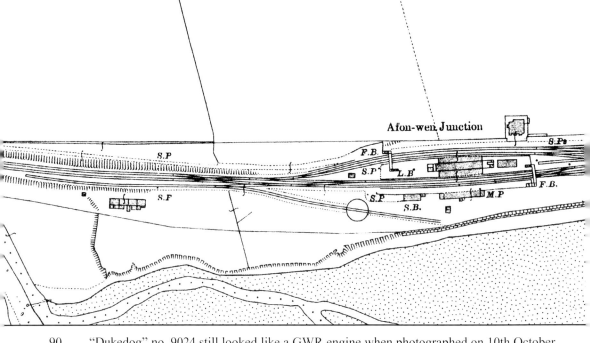

Afon-wen Junction

90.   "Dukedog" no. 9024 still looked like a GWR engine when photographed on 10th October 1951. On the right is the gate for the stationmaster to reach his dwelling, which is seen in picture 94. (H.Ballantyne)

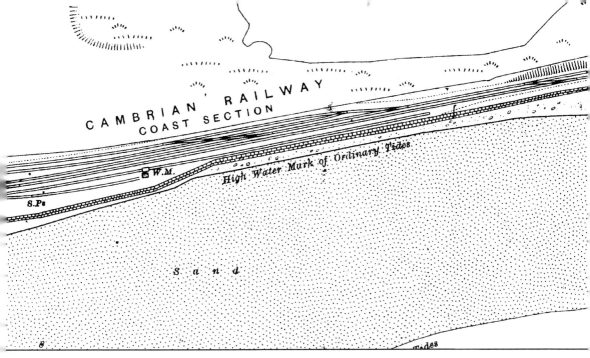

XXI.   The 1917 edition includes the position of the turntable, which lasted until the 1930s. Trains from Bangor used the upper line on the left and often the northern platform. There were ten men here for most of the 1930s.

91.   Two photographs from 22nd March 1962 enhance our survey. On the left, no. 42601 waits for the signal to leave for Pwllheli, while no. 42446 is at platform 1 with a short freight train for Bangor. Both are ex-LMS 2-6-4Ts. (M.A.N.Johnston)

92. The view towards Criccieth from the footbridge includes the two goods sidings, which ceased to be used after 4th November 1963. The route is close to the sea for about a mile. No. 42446 stands near the beach. (M.A.N.Johnston)

Afonwen	1923	1929	1930	1933
Passenger tickets issued	13631	6212	5635	13896
Season tickets issued	102	8	13	42
Parcels forwarded	148	134	148	152
General goods forwarded (tons)	2	2	1	29
Coal and coke received (tons)	-	-	-	-
Other minerals received (tons)	23	-	-	7
General goods received (tons)	16	5	3	1
Trucks of livestock handled	1	1	1	-

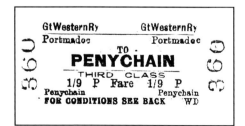

93.   Blowing off on 8th August 1964 is no. 75004 as it runs near the roofless gents. The tall post was fitted with a wire and winch for hoisting a pressurised oil lamp. (D.A.Johnson)

94.   Seen on the same day is Standard class 3 2-6-2T no. 82003 with the 10.44 to Pwllheli. This must have been a bad place to alight in a southwest gale. (D.A.Johnson)

95. The east end was recorded on 4th July 1965, along with the end of the goods siding. Passenger service was withdrawn on 7th December 1964, when the line closed to Carnarvon, as it was then. (D.K.Jones)

96. The west end and the entrance footbridge were photographed soon after the 75-lever signal box had closed on 30th April 1967. The track was double from here to Penychain from 3rd April 1947 until that date. No trace of this station remains. (Lens of Sutton coll.)

PENYCHAIN

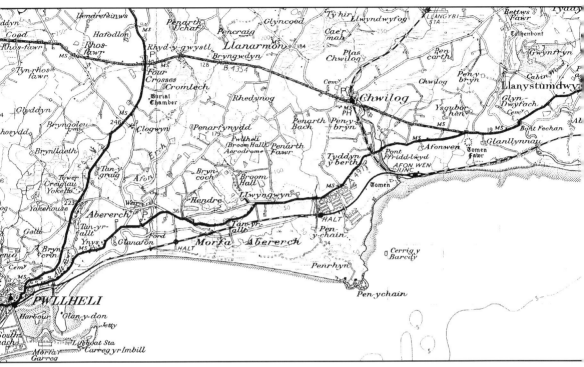

XXII. The Bangor line is at the top of this 1953 map at 1ins to 1 mile and Butlins Holiday Camp is to the left of Afon Wen Junction. The halt opened on 31st July 1933. Development of the camp was incomplete when World War II commenced, when it was requisitioned as a naval training base.

97.   The term "Halt" was dropped in 1947, when the line from Afon Wen was doubled. This view from 15th July 1965 includes the 13.15 Pwllheli to Dovey Junction class 101 DMU. Most of the visitors to the Camp had travelled on trains via Bangor. (C.L.Caddy)

98.   The 27-lever frame was in use from 3rd April 1947 to 30th April 1967. The box is seen in 1970. The station was named "Butlins" from 1993 to 2001. (C.L.Caddy)

99.   The platforms were photographed from the east in June 1970 and the view includes the ramp from the 1947 platform. Part of the original halt is evident; it has white coping. A five-car length was available in 2008. Local pronunciation is "Pen-er-kine". (C.L.Caddy)

ABERERCH

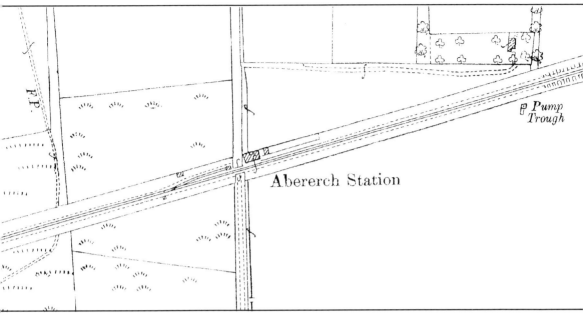

XXIII. The station was opened in July 1884 and is shown on the 1900 edition, also on the previous map.

100.   A 1961 westward panorama includes a camping coach in the siding and drinking water churns on the platform. The staff cottage is beyond the station building. The GWR first provided a "camp coach" in 1933. (Stations UK)

101.   A train for Pwllheli pulls in on the same day. Near the fire buckets is a set of portable steps, complete with handrails, for use by the less agile. The locomotive is no. 75026. (Stations UK)

102.   Pwllheli is in the distance in this record of the siding in about 1951. Goods traffic ceased and staffing came to an end on 1st May 1956. (R.S.Carpenter)

103.   The platform was still at a low level when a class 104 DMU bound for Pwllheli was photographed on 22nd June 1981. (T.Heavyside)

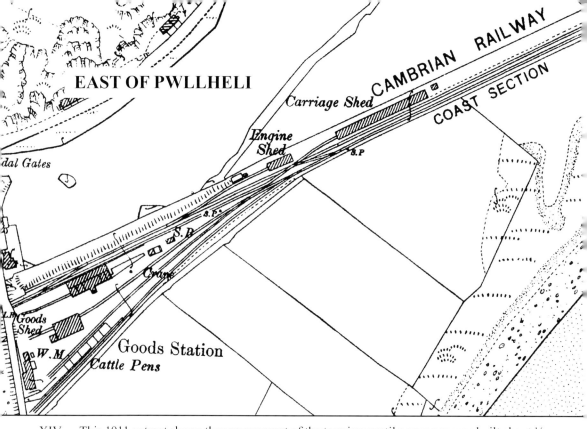

EAST OF PWLLHELI

Carriage Shed

Engine Shed

CAMBRIAN RAILWAY

COAST SECTION

dal Gates

S.P

S.P

S.B

Crane

L.B Goods Shed

W.M

Goods Station

Cattle Pens

XIV.   This 1911 extract shows the arrangement of the terminus until a new one was built about ½ mile to the west. It opened on 19th July 1909, which explains why "station" does not appear hereon. It was the building above the goods shed. The signal box had 18 levers and was in use until 1925.

104.   The sheds north of the running line were abandoned and this engine shed was built on the site of the passenger station. The down line is in the foreground, as 2-6-2T no. 5524 rests on 18th August 1953. (H.C.Casserley)

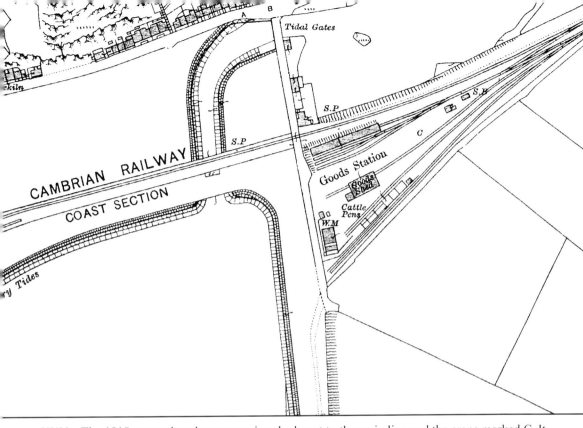

XXV. The 1918 survey has the new engine shed next to the main line and the crane marked C. It was listed as 6-ton capacity in 1938. On the left is the headshunt for the new station. Goods traffic continued until about 1975. The signal box had 18 levers and became Pwllheli East in 1909. It was rebuilt with 23 levers in 1925 and worked double track to the terminus from thereon.

105. No. 4549 stands with two classmates on 23rd July 1956. The turntable went to the West Somerset Railway and was installed at Minehead in 2008. The water tower is serving locomotives at Welshpool Raven Square. (G.Adams/M.J.Stretton coll.)

106.   The date is 25th August 1957 and class 2MT 2-6-2T no. 75020 is near the crane, with 2-6-2Ts no. 4549 and 4599 alongside. The level crossing was used by road traffic to the goods yard. (J.H.Morton/M.J.Stretton coll.)

107.   The old shed was in ruins by 1959 and was replaced then by this structure, recorded on 3rd July 1961. The 2-6-0 is no. 6339 of the 4300 class. There were 34 locomotive men here in January 1965, when the shed closed. It was later put to commercial use. (L.W.Rowe)

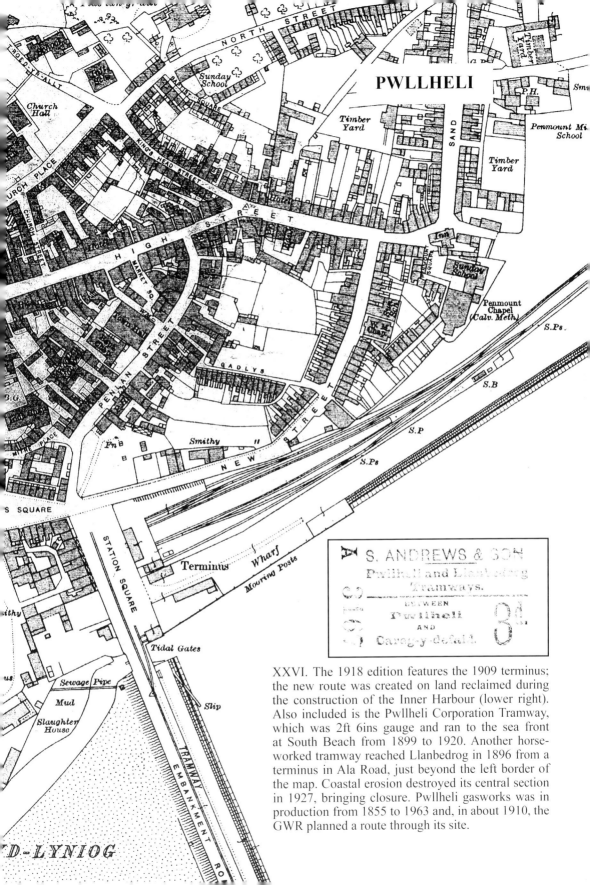

PWLLHELI

NORTH STREET

Sunday School

Church Hall

Church Place

Timber Yard

SAND

Penmount Mi. School

Timber Yard

P.H.

Sm.

Troed y allt

KING'S HEAD STREET

HIGH STREET

Hotel

Inn

Sunday School

S.Ps

Penmount Chapel (Calv. Meth.)

Church Street

Market Sq.

PENLAN STREET

GADLYS

NEW STREET

S.B

S.P

Mitre Place

Smithy

Fn B

S.Ps

B.G.

S SQUARE

Terminus   Wharf
Mooring Posts

STATION SQUARE

smithy

Sewage Pipe

Mud

Slaughter House

Tidal Gates

Slip

TRAMWAY EMBANKMENT ROAD

D-LYNIOG

XXVI. The 1918 edition features the 1909 terminus; the new route was created on land reclaimed during the construction of the Inner Harbour (lower right). Also included is the Pwllheli Corporation Tramway, which was 2ft 6ins gauge and ran to the sea front at South Beach from 1899 to 1920. Another horse-worked tramway reached Llanbedrog in 1896 from a terminus in Ala Road, just beyond the left border of the map. Coastal erosion destroyed its central section in 1927, bringing closure. Pwllheli gasworks was in production from 1855 to 1963 and, in about 1910, the GWR planned a route through its site.

108.   All goods traffic was handled at the original station site and so the presence of wagons here suggests that this view is from just prior to the opening of the station on 19th July 1909. (Stations UK)

109.   The extent of the Inner Harbour is revealed in this postcard panorama from the same time; it was a splendid vista for holidaymakers arriving by train. There was a total manpower of around 38 in the 1930s. (Lens of Sutton coll.)

110.   The spacious platform was designed to handle the crowds, but on this wet day in August 1951 there were few about for no. 42617 (left) to take to Bangor or no. 3201 to convey to Barmouth. (H.F.Wheeller/R.S.Carpenter coll.)

111.   The welcoming shelter of the canopy lasted well, but the glass had to be removed in 1979 and all was soon lost. The photograph is from about 1961, when the population was 3600. (Lens of Sutton coll.)

112.   The chalet style created a holiday ambiance and is seen in the same era, when two Fords had replaced a multitude of motor coaches destined for peaceful locations on the Lleyn Peninsula. (Lens of Sutton coll.)

113.   Pictured in June 1968, West Box had opened with the station and its 40 levers would function until 12th September 1976, when it became a ground frame. Each platform had an engine release road until that time. (C.L.Caddy)

↓ 114. A substantial number of Metro-Cammell class 101 DMUs were based at Machynlleth and this example was photographed on 13th May 1970. Cleaning was seldom undertaken in platforms by that time. (B.I.Nathan)

115. The original trackwork was still complete when the photographer arrived on 18th June 1977; so was the station. There were seven weekday departures to Barmouth or beyond, with trains to Porthmadog at 09.36 WO, 13.45 SO and 14.55 SX. The DMU is class 103. (R.A.Lumber/D.H.Mitchell coll.)

→ 116. The date is 22nd June 1981 and desolation had ensued. At least cover of the concourse had been retained, as had some staff. By that time, short journeys were limited to two to Criccieth, on Summer Wednesdays only. Here we have a class 104 DMU. (T.Heavyside)

Pwllheli	1923	1929	1930	1933
Passenger tickets issued	78925	48671	40969	38969
Season tickets issued	42	21	60	134
Parcels forwarded	64652	77362	76880	85354
General goods forwarded (tons)	989	3327	1122	1312
Coal and coke received (tons)	1215	1852	1435	1307
Other minerals received (tons)	4354	5603	6662	5665
General goods received (tons)	13134	14113	15129	13567
Trucks of livestock handled	703	655	677	567

117.   A servicing platform was added so that at least one side could be washed in private. No. 150116 is stabled, while nos 25201 and 25037 stand with a charter train from Paddington on 24th August 1986. (D.H.Mitchell)

118.   A supermarket had encroached on half the platform by August 1992, when class 31s were photographed with a special from Euston. The train will reverse to the loop for the engines to run round. (D.A.Johnson)

119. The Action Group's Sunday shuttle runs near West Box on 24th August 1986. Its frame had only four levers by that time and there was another ground frame on the site of East Box, as the up line had been retained as a loop. It is in the background. The line in the foreground is the siding on the right of picture 113. (D.H.Mitchell)

120. This is 6th May 2007 and being a Sunday it was possible to see a class 158 DMU in the siding, where they normally only rested at night. The platform could accommodate eight coaches and some regular steam services used it in the following Summer. (V.Mitchell)

MP Middleton Press

EVOLVING THE ULTIMATE RAIL ENCYCLOPEDIA

Easebourne Lane, Midhurst, West Sussex.
GU29 9AZ   Tel:01730 813169

www.middletonpress.co.uk   email:info@middletonpress.co.uk
A-978 0 906520   B- 978 1 873793   C- 978 1 901706   D-978 1 904474   E - 978 1 906008

OOP Out of print at time of printing - Please check availability   BROCHURE AVAILABLE SHOWING NEW TITLES